To my sisters, who are also my best friends,
Jill Swistak, Gina Schneider, and Linda Mammano

With special thanks to California Board Shop and James Adkins

ISBN 0-590-51508-X

Copyright © 1997 by Julie Mammano.
All rights reserved. Published by Scholastic Inc.,
555 Broadway, New York, NY 10012,
by arrangement with Chronicle Books.

SCHOLASTIC and associated logos are trademarks and/or registered trademarks of Scholastic Inc.

12 11 10 9 8 7 6 5 4 3 2 1   8 9/9 0 1 2 3/0

Printed in the U.S.A.   08

First Scholastic printing, September 1998

Book design by Lucy Nielsen. Typeset in Gil Sans.

JULIE MAMMANO

Rhinos Who Snowboard

SCHOLASTIC INC.
New York Toronto London Auckland Sydney

Rhinos who snowboard live for the snow.

They strap on their boards and take a lift to the GNARLIEST peaks.

They reach the top and . . . JUMP!

They BUST OUT fast down the FALL LINE!

They go **TOTALLY AGGRO.**

They **CHARGE** the steepest slopes.

They ride through the backcountry.

They carve perfect POWDER FANS.

Rhinos who snowboard FLOAT STIFFY TAILGRABS.

They catch PHAT AIR over INSANE GAPS.

They plant **HOHOS** off the lip of a windblown **HALFPIPE.**

Rhinos who snowboard are SPIN MASTERS.

They **LAUNCH MAJOR** backflips.

It is so UNCOOL when MOGUL hopping KOOKS botch up their big jumps.

Rhinos who snowboard HUCK over cliffs and have RUDE mid-air SLAMS.

At the end of the day, they take their final run.

Tomorrow will be
EPIC!

Board Speak

air jump trick

bonk to hit an object on purpose for style

bummer really bad

bust out to start quickly then go fast

charge go for it

chill out relax

dump to snowfall in big amounts

epic really great

faceplant to land on your face

fakie to ride backwards

fall line straight down a slope of a mountain

float to make a big jump

freefall to fall airborne straight down

gnarliest biggest, scariest

halfpipe curve in snow shaped like a tube

hohos two handed handstands

huck to jump wildly

insane gaps big spaces between cliffs or slopes

kooks jerks who ski or snowboard

pow powdery snow

powder fans snow sprayed in the shape of a fan

rude really bad

slams crashes

spin master one who does spin tricks

stiffy with both legs straight

stoked to the max really happy

tailgrabs grab the back of the board

totally aggro fearless

uncool bad

launch to take off on a jump

major very

mogul bump in the snow

phat really big, high, or great

poser pretend snowboarder